AF227689

This book belongs to:

~~~~~~~~~~~~~~~~~~~~~~

a Warrior Scholar

Kamali Academy

Kamali Academy strives to help warrior parents across the globe provide their young warrior scholars with an education for liberation. This workbook is apart of that continued mission.

Young warrior scholars can use this book and its mental math tips to master basic and advanced division thoroughly and quickly.

Whether you are homeschooling your child or supplementing the education they receive in the public and private school system, this will serve you well.

Parents, be sure to monitor the progress of your warrior scholar and watch them grow.

cover design:
Indigenous Lens
~~~~~~~~~~~~~~~~~~~~~~

FRACTIONS

Table of Contents:

Name: Date: /   /

1 **Understand:**

A fraction represents a part of a whole.

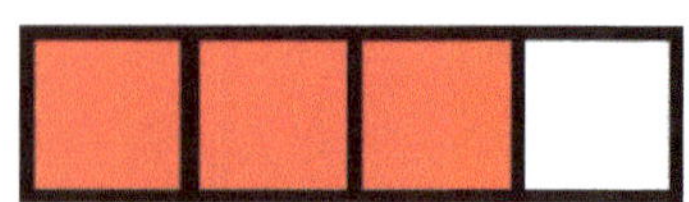

$$\frac{3}{4}$$

part / whole

Part of a whole can be named with a **fraction.** A fraction is written with two numbers. The bottom number of a fraction is called the **denominator.** The denominator tells *how many equal parts are in the whole.*

The top number of a fraction is called the **numerator.** The numerator tells *how many of the parts are being counted.* When naming a fraction, we name the numerator first; then we name the denominator using its ordinal number.

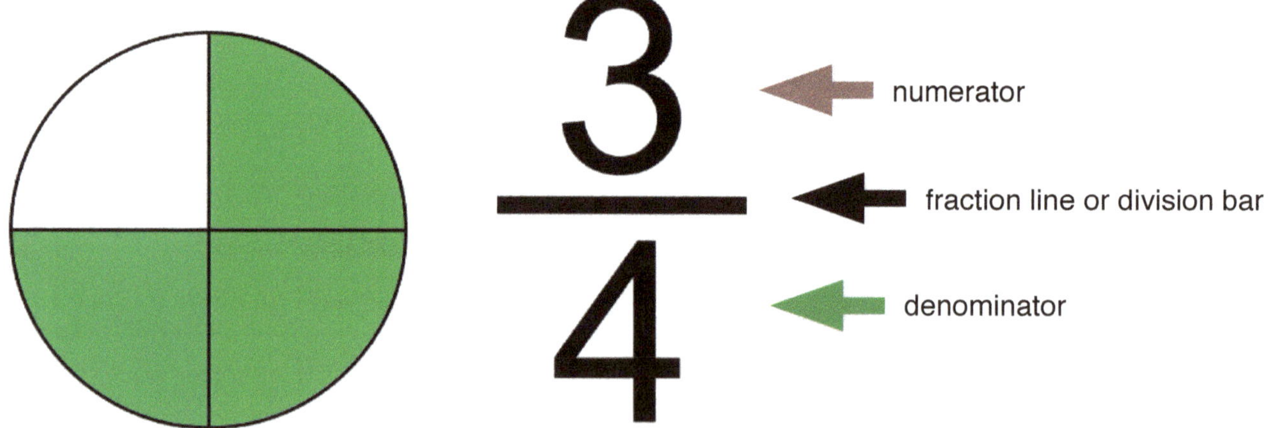

This fraction would be called three fourths.

(1) 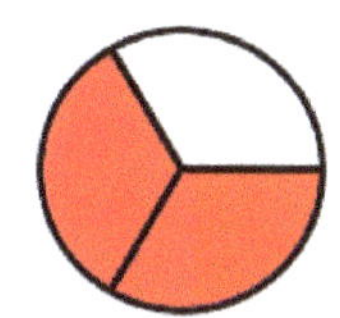 $\dfrac{2}{3}$

(2) 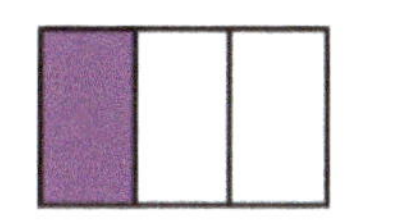 ___

(3) 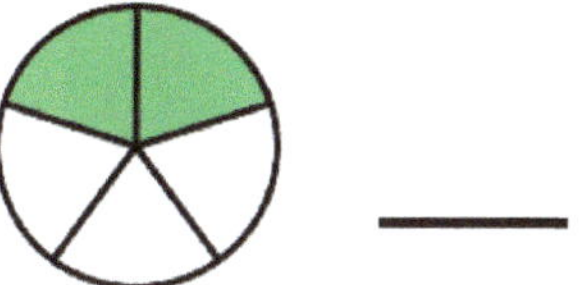 ___

(4)  ___

(5) 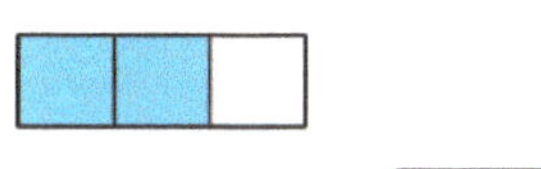 ___

(6) 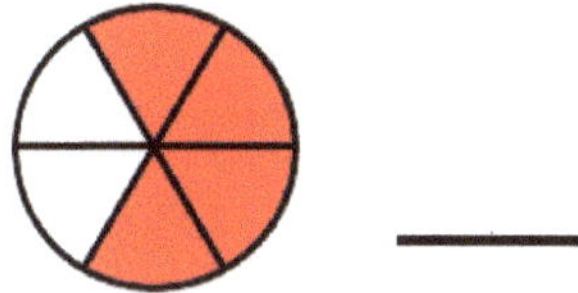 ___

(7) 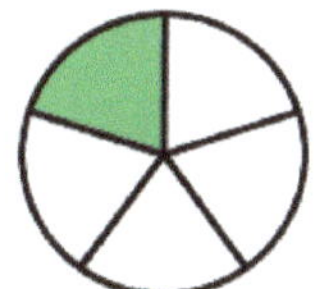 ___

(8)  ___

(9)  ___

(10) 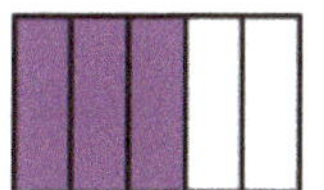 ___

(11) 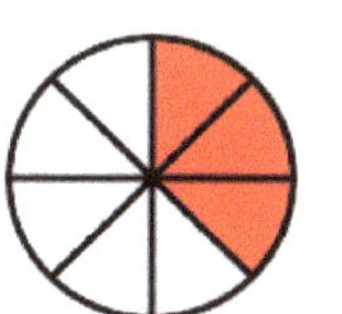 ___

(12)  ___

(13)  ___

(14) 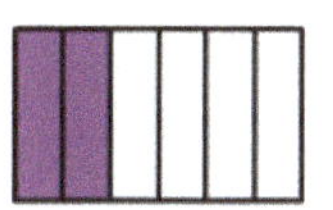 ___

(15) 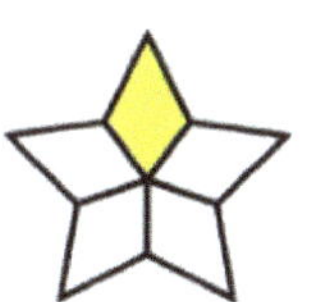 ___

(1) 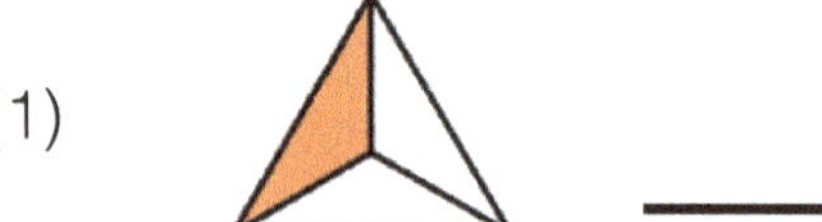 _____ (2)  _____ (3) 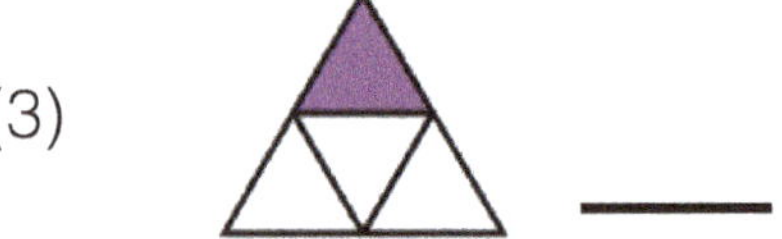 _____

(4) _____ (5) _____ (6) 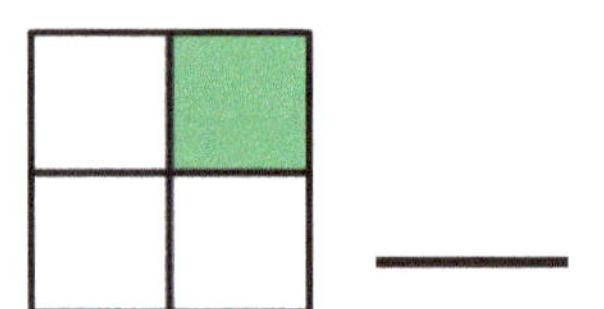 _____

(7) _____ (8) _____ (9) 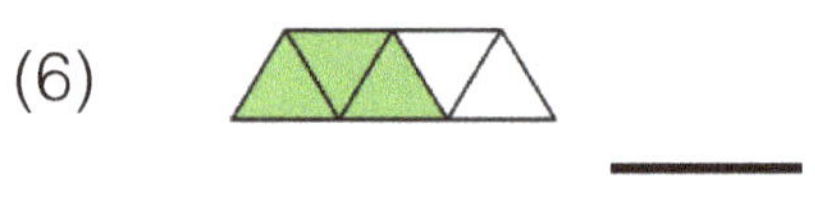 _____

(10) _____ (11) _____ (12) 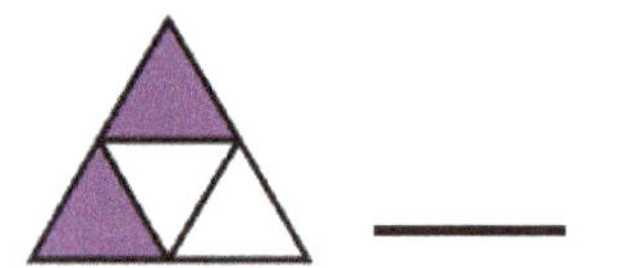 _____

(13) _____ (14) _____ (15) 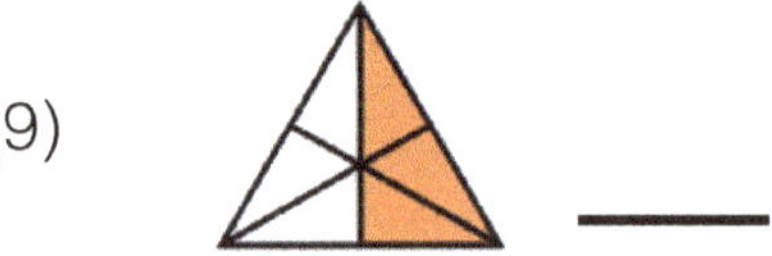 _____

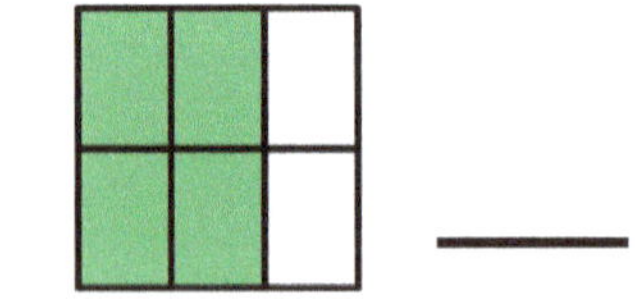
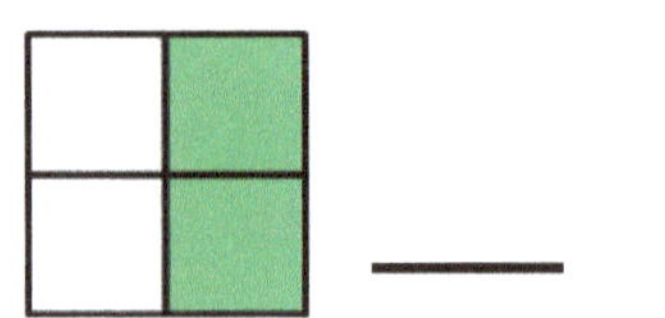
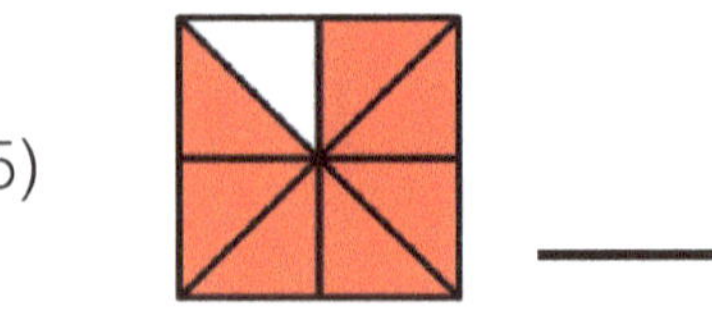

(1) What is the numerator of the fraction $\frac{4}{6}$? _____

(2) What is the denominator of the fraction $\frac{7}{9}$? _____

(3) What is the numerator of the fraction $\frac{9}{3}$? _____

(4) What is the denominator of the fraction $\frac{6}{7}$? _____

(5) What is the denominator of the fraction $\frac{5}{4}$? _____

(6) What is the denominator of the fraction $\frac{5}{9}$? _____

(7) What is the numerator of the fraction $\frac{2}{3}$? _____

(8) What is the numerator of the fraction $\frac{4}{5}$? _____

(9) What is the denominator of the fraction $\frac{1}{8}$? _____

(10) What is the denominator of the fraction $\frac{2}{1}$? _____

(11) What is the numerator of the fraction $\frac{8}{6}$? _____

(12) What is the numerator of the fraction $\frac{3}{6}$? _____

(13) What is the numerator of the fraction $\frac{3}{5}$? _____

(14) What is the denominator of the fraction $\frac{11}{8}$? _____

(15) What is the denominator of the fraction $\frac{4}{2}$? _____

(16) What is the denominator of the fraction $\frac{2}{8}$? _____

(17) What is the denominator of the fraction $\frac{3}{4}$? _____

(18) What is the denominator of the fraction $\frac{2}{4}$? _____

(19) What is the numerator of the fraction $\frac{4}{7}$? _____

(20) What is the numerator of the fraction $\frac{1}{4}$? _____

(21) What is the numerator of the fraction $\frac{8}{3}$? _____

(22) What is the denominator of the fraction $\frac{6}{8}$? _____

(23) What is the numerator of the fraction $\frac{5}{10}$? _____

(24) What is the numerator of the fraction $\frac{7}{9}$? _____

(25) What is the denominator of the fraction $\frac{4}{8}$? _____

(26) What is the numerator of the fraction $\frac{7}{5}$? _____

Name: Date: / /

1 **Practice:** Draw a picture to represent each fraction.

(1) $\frac{1}{2}$ 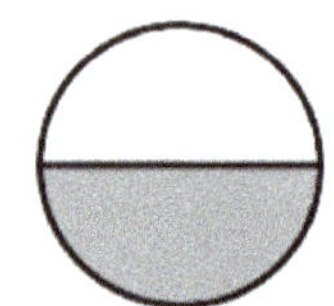

(2) $\frac{1}{3}$

(3) $\frac{1}{4}$

(4) $\frac{2}{5}$

(5) $\frac{1}{6}$

(6) $\frac{2}{4}$

(7) $\frac{0}{3}$

(8) $\frac{2}{9}$

(9) $\frac{5}{6}$

(10) $\frac{3}{4}$

(11) $\frac{9}{10}$

(12) $\frac{1}{8}$

2 **Practice:** Draw a picture to represent each fraction.

(1) $\dfrac{1}{1}$

(2) $\dfrac{3}{3}$

(3) $\dfrac{4}{6}$

(4) $\dfrac{4}{12}$

(5) $\dfrac{5}{10}$

(6) $\dfrac{4}{9}$

(7) $\dfrac{8}{12}$

(8) $\dfrac{4}{8}$

(9) $\dfrac{5}{16}$

(10) $\dfrac{1}{8}$

(11) $\dfrac{2}{5}$

(12) $\dfrac{6}{7}$

9

Name: Date: /   /

You can use words to refer to a part of a whole. So one whole has:

2 halves	6 sixths	10 tenths
3 thirds	7 sevenths	11 elevenths
4 quarters	8 eighths	12 twelfths
5 fifths	9 ninths	13 thirteenths

The fraction $\dfrac{3}{4}$

can be written in words as: **three quarters**

1 **Practice:** Write the following fractions in words:

(1) $\dfrac{2}{3}$ _______________

(2) $\dfrac{1}{10}$ _______________

(3) $\dfrac{1}{2}$ _______________

(4) $\dfrac{3}{7}$ _______________

(5) $\dfrac{4}{5}$ _______________

(6) $\dfrac{8}{12}$ _______________

(7) $\dfrac{8}{9}$ _______________

(8) $\dfrac{5}{6}$ _______________

(9) $\dfrac{5}{8}$ _______________

(10) $\dfrac{2}{5}$ _______________

(11) $\dfrac{6}{12}$ _______________

(12) $\dfrac{7}{10}$ _______________

(13) $\dfrac{2}{9}$ _______________

(14) $\dfrac{2}{6}$ _______________

(15) $\dfrac{11}{12}$ _______________

(16) $\dfrac{5}{7}$ _______________

(1) one third _________

(2) one half _________

(3) one sixth _________

(4) two fifths _________

(5) four sevenths _________

(6) seven eighths _________

(7) five twelfths _________

(8) eight ninths _________

(9) six tenths _________

(10) eight sixths _________

(11) seven twelfths _________

(12) one fifth _________

(13) one eleventh _______

(14) eight ninths _______

(15) six tenths _______

(16) six twelfths _______

(17) five sixths _______

(18) two sevenths _______

(19) two thirds _______

(20) five thirteenths _______

Name: Date: /   /

1. A fraction is nothing but a division question.

2. The dividend (numerator) represents how many parts are taken.
The divisor (denominator) represents the number of equal parts into which the whole is divided.

$$\frac{3}{4}$$

The dividend (numerator) is 3.
The divisor (denominator) is 4.
The fraction in words is three quarters.

A possible picture representation of this fraction is:

1 **Practice:** Fill out the following table:

	Fractions	Numerator (Dividend)	Denominator (Divisor)	The fraction written in words	Picture representation
1	$\frac{2}{3}$	2	3	two thirds	
2		1	4		
3				three fifths	
4					
5		3			
6	$\frac{}{5}$	2			
7	$\frac{3}{}$		5		

⑤ Understanding Mixed Numbers

Name: _______________ Date: ___ / ___ / ___

A mixed number is an addition of wholes and a part of a whole.

There are one complete whole and three quarters of the second whole

whole-number part (the number of complete wholes)

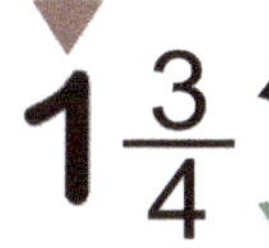

$1\dfrac{3}{4}$

★ The fraction can be written in words as *one and three quarters.*

The *numerator* indicates how many parts are taken from the last whole.

The *denominator* represents the number of equal parts into which the whole is divided.

① Practice: Write the mixed number that corresponds to the shaded region:

(1)  ______

(2) 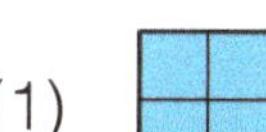 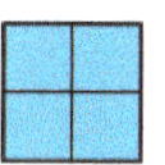 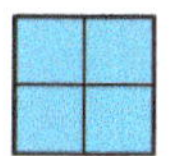  ______

(3) 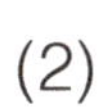 ______

(4) 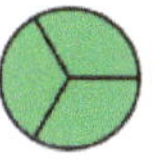 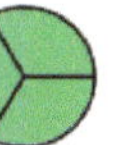 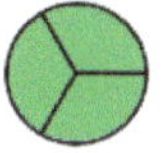 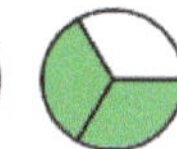 ______

(5) 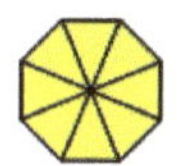  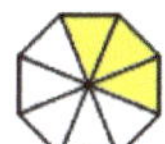 ______

(6) 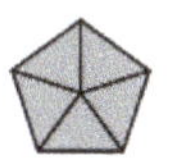  ______

(7) 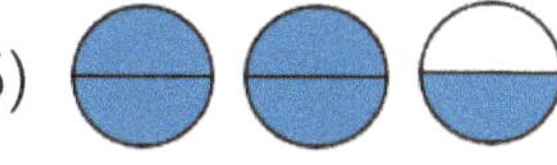 ______

(8) 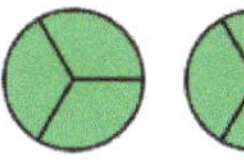 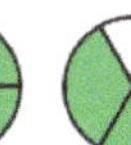 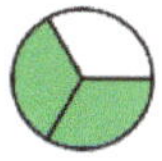 ______

(9)   ______

(10) 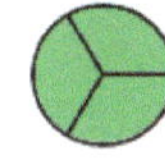 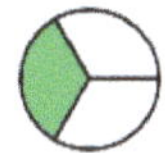 ______

(11)  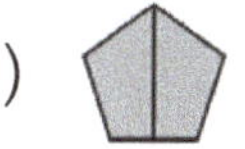   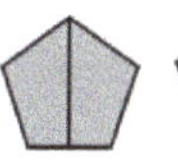  ______

(12)      ______

(13) 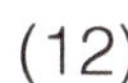 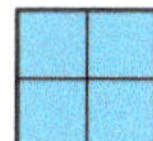  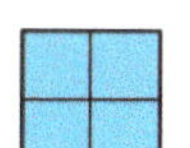  ______

(14) 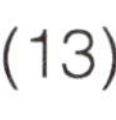 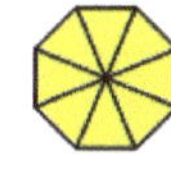 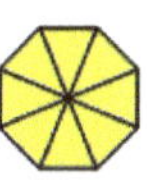  ______

(15) 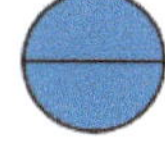  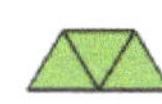 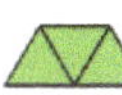 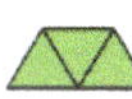 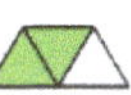 ______

(16)       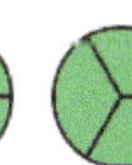 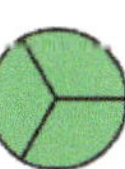  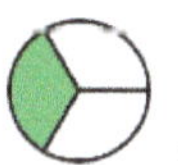 ______

 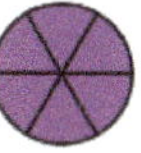 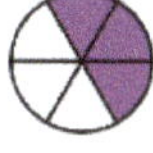 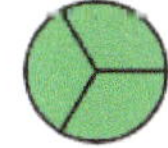 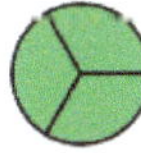  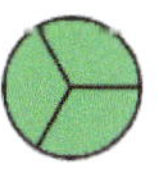 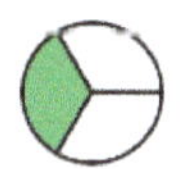 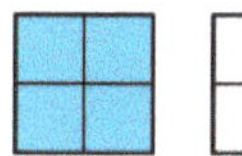 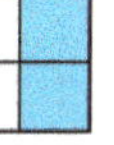

Kamali Academy Fractions

(1) $2\frac{2}{3}$ _______________

(2) $5\frac{1}{10}$ _______________

(3) $8\frac{1}{2}$ _______________

(4) $3\frac{3}{7}$ _______________

(5) $5\frac{4}{5}$ _______________

(6) $1\frac{8}{12}$ _______________

(7) $2\frac{8}{9}$ _______________

(8) $7\frac{5}{6}$ _______________

(9) $1\frac{5}{8}$ _______________

(10) $3\frac{2}{5}$ _______________

(11) $7\frac{6}{12}$ _______________

(12) $1\frac{7}{10}$ _______________

(13) $8\frac{2}{9}$ _______________

(14) $2\frac{2}{6}$ _______________

(15) $8\frac{11}{12}$ _______________

(16) $1\frac{5}{7}$ _______________

#	Mixed number	Number of wholes	Numerator	Denominator	The mixed number in words	Graphical representation
1	$2\frac{3}{5}$	2	3	5	two and three fifths	
2	$2\frac{1}{3}$					
3		1	3	4		
4						
5	$2\frac{\ }{5}$		3			
6	$3\frac{2}{\ }$			5		
7	$\frac{2}{3}$	2				

Fractions on the Number line

6

Name: ___________ Date: ___ / ___ / ___

Fractions can also be shown on a number line.

The red dot is at 2/4 on the number line.

Count the number of segments between 0 and 1. There are 4 segments or spaces.

1 **Practice:** Identify the fractions on the number line. Circle your answer.

Which point is at $\frac{1}{3}$ on the number line?

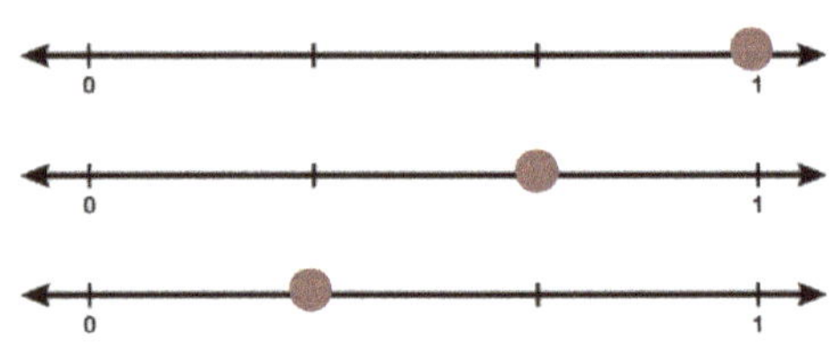

Which point is at $\frac{3}{8}$ on the number line?

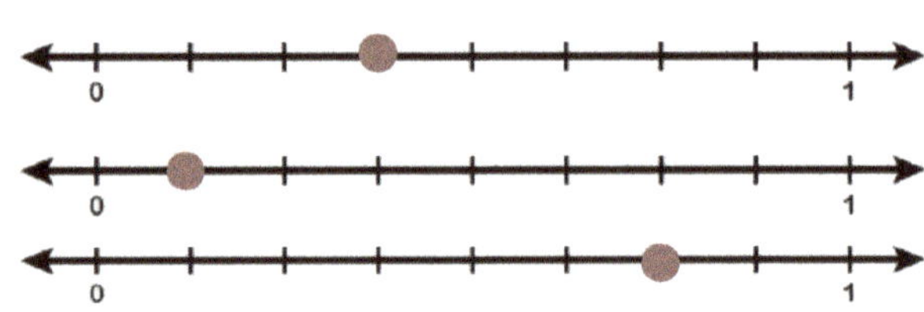

Which point is at $\frac{2}{5}$ on the number line?

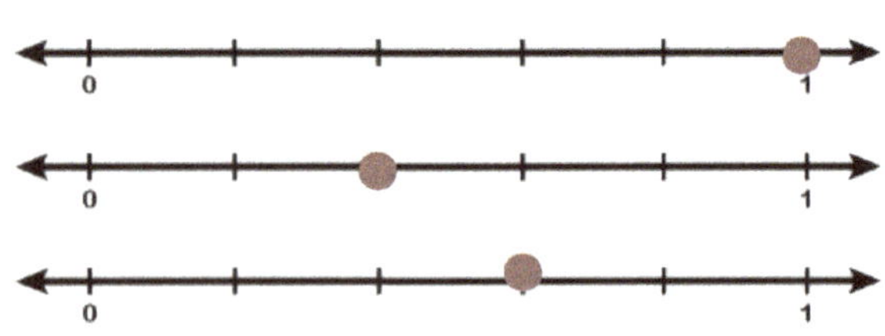

Which point is at $\frac{3}{4}$ on the number line?

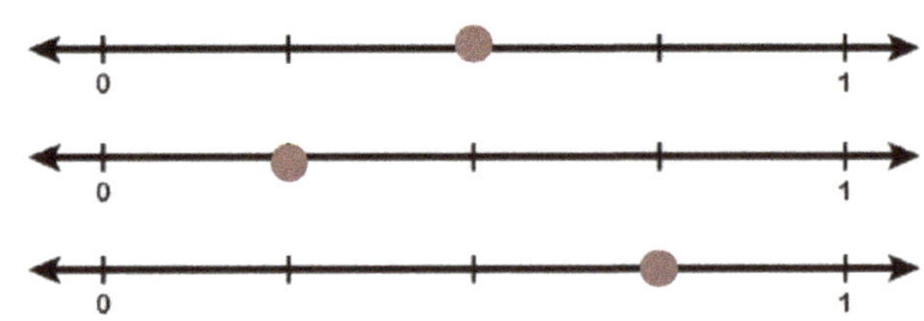

Which point is at $\frac{1}{2}$ on the number line?

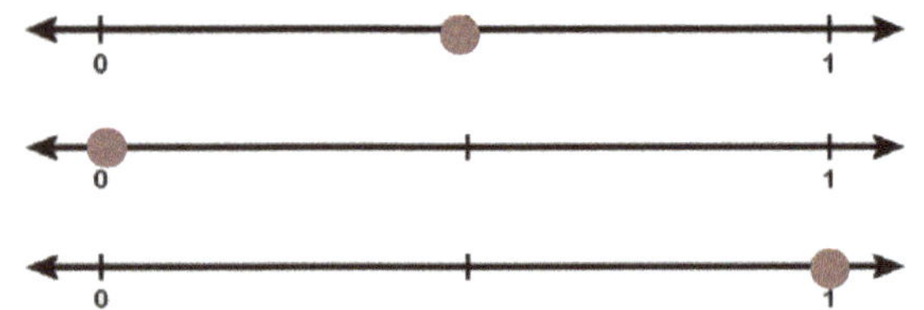

Which point is at $\frac{4}{9}$ on the number line?

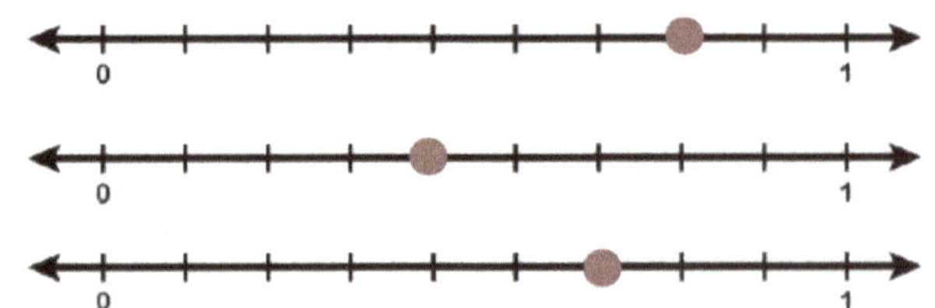

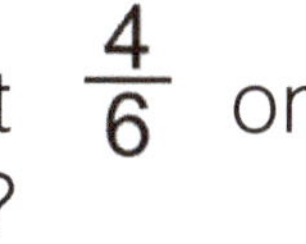 **Practice:** Identify the fractions on the number line. Circle your answer.

Which point is at $\dfrac{4}{6}$ on the number line?

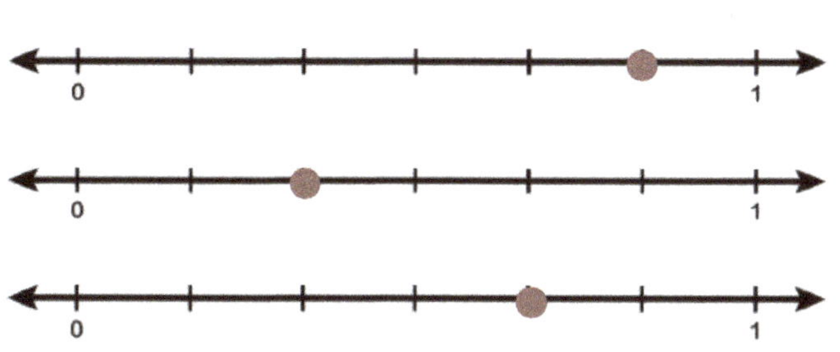

Which point is at $\dfrac{3}{7}$ on the number line?

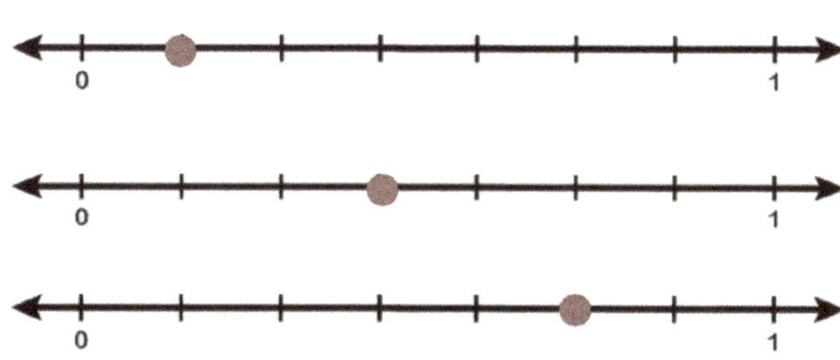

Which point is at $\dfrac{6}{8}$ on the number line?

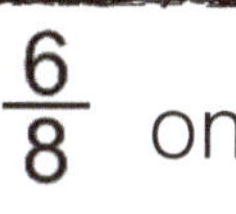

Which point is at $\dfrac{7}{7}$ on the number line?

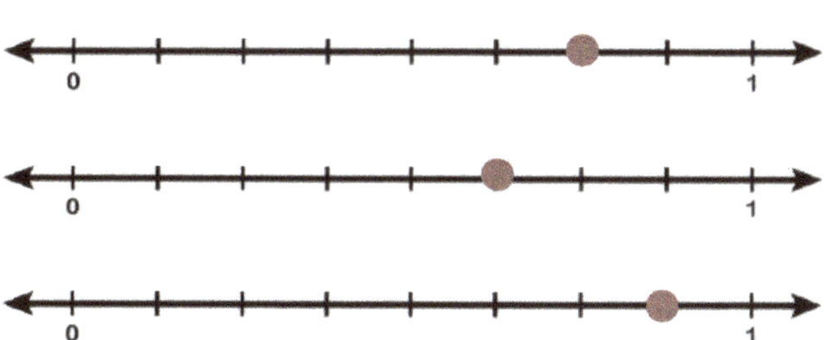

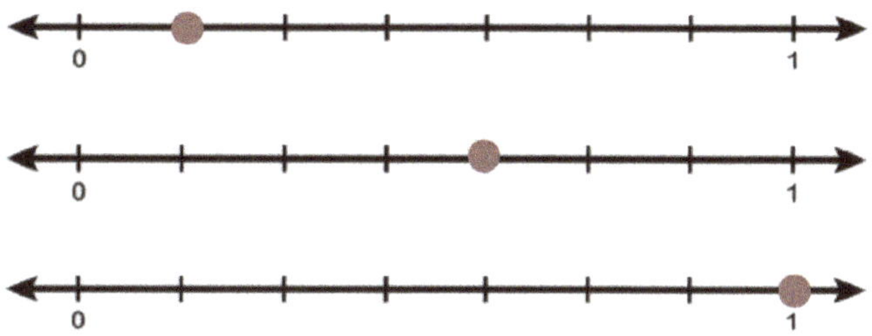

Which point is at $\dfrac{3}{6}$ on the number line?

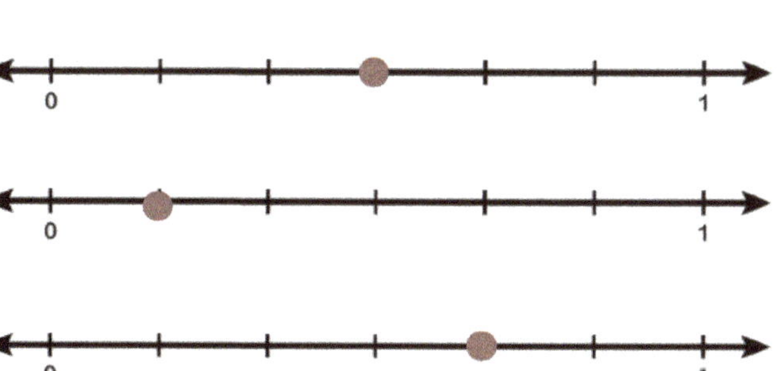

Which point is at $\dfrac{1}{5}$ on the number line?

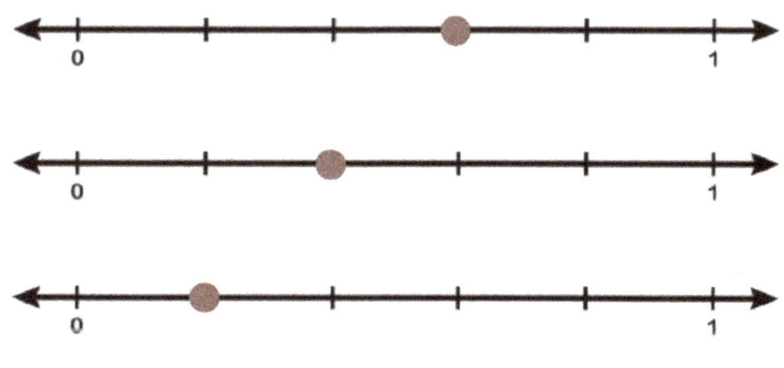

Equivalent Fractions

Name: ___________   Date: /   /

Equivalent fractions are different names for the same number. $\dfrac{1}{2}, \dfrac{2}{4}, \dfrac{3}{6}, \dfrac{4}{8}$ ← all the fractions are equivalent.

To find equivalent fractions, we multiply a number by different fraction names for 1. $\dfrac{1}{2} \times \dfrac{3}{3} = \dfrac{3}{6}$

1 **Practice:** Find the fraction name for 1 used to make each equivalent fractions.

(1) $\dfrac{3}{4} \times \dfrac{?}{?} = \dfrac{9}{12}$ $\dfrac{3}{3}$ _______

(2) $\dfrac{2}{3} \times \dfrac{?}{?} = \dfrac{4}{6}$ _______

(3) $\dfrac{1}{3} \times \dfrac{?}{?} = \dfrac{4}{12}$ _______

(4) $\dfrac{1}{4} \times \dfrac{?}{?} = \dfrac{5}{20}$ _______

(5) $\dfrac{5}{8} \times \dfrac{?}{?} = \dfrac{10}{16}$ _______

(6) $\dfrac{2}{6} \times \dfrac{?}{?} = \dfrac{4}{12}$ _______

(7) $\dfrac{1}{5} \times \dfrac{?}{?} = \dfrac{4}{20}$ _______

(8) $\dfrac{4}{8} \times \dfrac{?}{?} = \dfrac{8}{16}$ _______

(9) $\dfrac{1}{2} \times \dfrac{?}{?} = \dfrac{5}{10}$ _______

(10) $\dfrac{3}{8} \times \dfrac{?}{?} = \dfrac{6}{16}$ _______

(11) $\dfrac{4}{5} \times \dfrac{?}{?} = \dfrac{12}{15}$ _______

(12) $\dfrac{2}{3} \times \dfrac{?}{?} = \dfrac{8}{12}$ _______

Practice: Find the missing number.

(1)
$$\frac{2}{3} = \frac{?}{15} \qquad ? = \underline{}$$

(2)
$$\frac{3}{5} = \frac{?}{10} \qquad ? = \underline{}$$

(3)
$$\frac{1}{3} = \frac{3}{?} \qquad ? = \underline{}$$

(4)
$$\frac{1}{6} = \frac{?}{12} \qquad ? = \underline{}$$

(5)
$$\frac{2}{8} = \frac{?}{16} \qquad ? = \underline{}$$

(6)
$$\frac{9}{12} = \frac{?}{4} \qquad ? = \underline{}$$

(7)
$$\frac{2}{10} = \frac{1}{?} \qquad ? = \underline{}$$

(8)
$$\frac{4}{8} = \frac{8}{?} \qquad ? = \underline{}$$

(9)
$$\frac{6}{20} = \frac{3}{?} \qquad ? = \underline{}$$

(10)
$$\frac{12}{16} = \frac{3}{?} \qquad ? = \underline{}$$

(11)
$$\frac{1}{2} = \frac{?}{16} \qquad ? = \underline{}$$

(12)
$$\frac{2}{3} = \frac{?}{6} \qquad ? = \underline{}$$

Name: ___________   Date: / /

$$\frac{4}{9} < \frac{4}{5}$$

$\frac{4}{9}$ 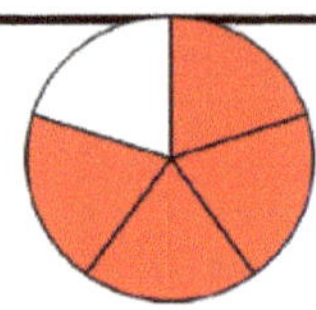 $\frac{4}{5}$

It is clear that the **4 pieces in 4/5 is larger than the 4 pieces in 4/9.**

To compare fractions, we use the **<, >**, and **=** signs.

With the same numerator, drawing pictures can help.

When the denominators are the same, **we compare the two numerators to get the answer.**

$$\frac{4}{6} < \frac{5}{6}$$

 **Practice:** Compare the Fractions using <, >, or =

(1) $\frac{3}{3} \bigcirc \frac{3}{8}$

(2) $\frac{5}{6} \bigcirc \frac{3}{6}$

(3) $\frac{1}{8} \bigcirc \frac{1}{4}$

(4) $\frac{3}{8} \bigcirc \frac{7}{8}$

---

(5) $\frac{1}{3} \bigcirc \frac{1}{4}$

(6) $\frac{4}{4} \bigcirc \frac{1}{4}$

(7) $\frac{1}{4} \bigcirc \frac{1}{3}$

(8) $\frac{3}{3} \bigcirc \frac{2}{3}$

---

(9) $\frac{2}{3} \bigcirc \frac{2}{2}$

(10) $\frac{3}{3} \bigcirc \frac{1}{3}$

(11) $\frac{4}{4} \bigcirc \frac{4}{6}$

(12) $\frac{6}{8} \bigcirc \frac{1}{8}$

---

(13) $\frac{2}{2} \bigcirc \frac{2}{4}$

(14) $\frac{1}{3} \bigcirc \frac{2}{3}$

(15) $\frac{3}{8} \bigcirc \frac{3}{3}$

(16) $\frac{2}{4} \bigcirc \frac{2}{6}$

Name: ____________   Date: ___/___/___

$\frac{3}{4} \bigcirc \frac{7}{8}$

Rewriting fractions with common denominators can help us compare fractions.

$\frac{3}{4} \times \frac{2}{2} = \frac{6}{8}$

Change 4, the denominator in 3/4, to 8 by multiplying by 2/2.

$\frac{6}{8} \enclose{circle}{<} \frac{7}{8}$

Now, we see that 6/8 is less than 7/8.

$$\frac{3}{4} < \frac{7}{8}$$

---

1 **Practice:** Compare the Fractions using <, >, or =

(1) $\frac{1}{4} \bigcirc \frac{3}{5}$

(2) $\frac{3}{4} \bigcirc \frac{6}{8}$

(3) $\frac{1}{5} \bigcirc \frac{4}{6}$

(4) $\frac{4}{8} \bigcirc \frac{7}{10}$

---

(5) $\frac{7}{12} \bigcirc \frac{1}{2}$

(6) $\frac{2}{3} \bigcirc \frac{1}{5}$

(7) $\frac{3}{10} \bigcirc \frac{1}{6}$

(8) $\frac{4}{10} \bigcirc \frac{1}{5}$

---

(9) $\frac{4}{5} \bigcirc \frac{6}{8}$

(10) $\frac{2}{4} \bigcirc \frac{1}{2}$

(11) $\frac{3}{4} \bigcirc \frac{5}{10}$

(12) $\frac{1}{12} \bigcirc \frac{4}{8}$

---

(13) $\frac{1}{3} \bigcirc \frac{6}{8}$

(14) $\frac{2}{3} \bigcirc \frac{1}{2}$

(15) $\frac{3}{4} \bigcirc \frac{7}{8}$

(16) $\frac{2}{6} \bigcirc \frac{2}{4}$

$$\frac{1}{2} = 50\% \quad .50$$

$$\frac{1}{3} = 33\% \quad .33$$

$$\frac{2}{3} = 66\% \quad .66$$

$$\frac{1}{4} = 25\% \quad .25$$

$$\frac{2}{4} = 50\% \quad .50$$

$$\frac{3}{4} = 75\% \quad .75$$

$$\frac{1}{5} = 20\% \quad .20$$

$$\frac{2}{5} = 40\% \quad .40$$

$$\frac{3}{5} = 60\% \quad .60$$

$$\frac{4}{5} = 80\% \quad .80$$

$$\frac{1}{6} = 16\% \quad .16$$

$$\frac{2}{6} = 33\% \quad .33$$

$$\frac{3}{6} = 50\% \quad .50$$

$$\frac{4}{6} = 66\% \quad .66$$

$$\frac{5}{6} = 83\% \quad .83$$

$$\frac{1}{7} = 14\% \quad .14$$

$$\frac{2}{7} = 28\% \quad .28$$

$$\frac{3}{7} = 42\% \quad .42$$

$$\frac{4}{7} = 57\% \quad .57$$

$$\frac{5}{7} = 71\% \quad .71$$

$$\frac{6}{7} = 85\% \quad .85$$

$$\frac{1}{8} = 33\% \quad .33$$

$$\frac{2}{8} = 66\% \quad .66$$

$$\frac{3}{8} = 25\% \quad .25$$

$$\frac{4}{8} = 50\% \quad .50$$

$$\frac{5}{8} = 75\% \quad .75$$

$$\frac{6}{8} = 20\% \quad .20$$

$$\frac{7}{8} = 40\% \quad .40$$

When studying these fractions, be sure to look for patterns that will help you remember.

$\dfrac{1}{9}$ = 11% .11

$\dfrac{2}{9}$ = 22% .22

$\dfrac{3}{9}$ = 33% .33

$\dfrac{4}{9}$ = 44% .44

$\dfrac{5}{9}$ = 55% .55

$\dfrac{6}{9}$ = 66% .66

$\dfrac{7}{9}$ = 77% .77

$\dfrac{8}{9}$ = 88% .88

$\dfrac{1}{10}$ = 10% .10

$\dfrac{2}{10}$ = 20% .20

$\dfrac{3}{10}$ = 30% .30

$\dfrac{4}{10}$ = 40% .40

$\dfrac{5}{10}$ = 50% .50

$\dfrac{6}{10}$ = 60% .60

$\dfrac{7}{10}$ = 70% .70

$\dfrac{8}{10}$ = 80% .80

$\dfrac{9}{10}$ = 90% .90

$\dfrac{1}{11}$ = 9% .09

$\dfrac{2}{11}$ = 18% .18

$\dfrac{3}{11}$ = 27% .27

$\dfrac{4}{11}$ = 36% .36

$\dfrac{5}{11}$ = 45% .45

$\dfrac{6}{11}$ = 54% .54

$\dfrac{7}{11}$ = 63% .63

$\dfrac{8}{11}$ = 72% .72

$\dfrac{9}{11}$ = 81% .81

$\dfrac{10}{11}$ = 90% .90

When studying these fractions, be sure to look for patterns that will help you remember.

  Kamali Academy Fractions

Name: _______________   Date: /   /

To simplify a fractions, you must find the greatest common factor of both numbers.
Then, divide each number by that factor to get a simpler fraction.

$$\frac{8}{16} \begin{array}{c}\div\ 8\\ \div\ 8\end{array} = \frac{1}{2}$$

Find the greatest common factor.

*hint: if the numbers are even, two is definitely a factor. Start there if you need to.

1 **Practice:** Simplify the fractions.

(1) $\dfrac{2}{4}$ ______

(2) $\dfrac{5}{15}$ ______

(5) $\dfrac{12}{24}$ ______

(6) $\dfrac{14}{18}$ ______

(3) $\dfrac{6}{14}$ ______

(4) $\dfrac{21}{28}$ ______

(7) $\dfrac{10}{35}$ ______

(8) $\dfrac{9}{15}$ ______

(9) $\dfrac{56}{49}$ ______

(10) $\dfrac{72}{63}$ ______

(13) $\dfrac{45}{30}$ ______

(14) $\dfrac{18}{30}$ ______

(11) $\dfrac{14}{35}$ ______

(12) $\dfrac{28}{63}$ ______

(15) $\dfrac{60}{48}$ ______

(16) $\dfrac{81}{45}$ ______

(17) $\dfrac{18}{54}$ ______

(18) $\dfrac{36}{48}$ ______

(21) $\dfrac{9}{90}$ ______

(22) $\dfrac{40}{32}$ ______

(19) $\dfrac{100}{25}$ ______

(20) $\dfrac{24}{39}$ ______

(23) $\dfrac{45}{27}$ ______

(24) $\dfrac{15}{45}$ ______

Adding and Subtracting Fractions with Same Denominators

Name: ___________   Date: /   /

When fractions have common denominators, *we can add or subtract the fractions by simply adding or subtracting the numerators*. We do not add or subtract the denominators.

$$\frac{2}{4} + \frac{1}{4} = \frac{3}{4}$$

add the numerators
remains unchanged

$$\frac{5}{10} - \frac{3}{10} = \frac{2}{10}$$

subtract the numerators
remains unchanged

---

1   **Practice:** Simplify the fractions.

(1) $\dfrac{2}{8} + \dfrac{3}{8} =$ _______

(2) $\dfrac{1}{9} + \dfrac{3}{9} =$ _______

(3) $\dfrac{4}{5} - \dfrac{1}{5} =$ _______

(4) $\dfrac{4}{7} - \dfrac{2}{7} =$ _______

(5) $\dfrac{2}{6} + \dfrac{3}{6} =$ _______

(6) $\dfrac{3}{4} - \dfrac{1}{4} =$ _______

(7) $\dfrac{3}{12} + \dfrac{4}{12} =$ _______

(8) $\dfrac{1}{3} + \dfrac{1}{3} =$ _______

(9) $\dfrac{1}{7} + \dfrac{5}{7} =$ _______

(10) $\dfrac{4}{8} + \dfrac{5}{8} =$ _______

(11) $\dfrac{5}{10} + \dfrac{5}{10} =$ _______

(12) $\dfrac{4}{15} + \dfrac{6}{15} =$ _______

(1) $\dfrac{3}{4} + \dfrac{5}{4} =$ _______

(2) $\dfrac{2}{12} + \dfrac{3}{12} =$ _______

(3) $\dfrac{2}{3} + \dfrac{1}{3} =$ _______

(4) $\dfrac{1}{3} + \dfrac{1}{3} =$ _______

(5) $\dfrac{2}{6} + \dfrac{1}{6} =$ _______

(6) $\dfrac{5}{3} + \dfrac{5}{3} =$ _______

(7) $\dfrac{5}{4} + \dfrac{6}{4} =$ _______

(8) $\dfrac{2}{8} + \dfrac{6}{8} =$ _______

(9) $\dfrac{5}{2} + \dfrac{6}{2} =$ _______

(10) $\dfrac{1}{12} + \dfrac{3}{12} =$ _______

(11) $\dfrac{1}{5} + \dfrac{4}{5} =$ _______

(12) $\dfrac{7}{9} + \dfrac{4}{9} =$ _______

(1) $\dfrac{4}{6} - \dfrac{1}{6} =$ _______

(2) $\dfrac{3}{4} - \dfrac{2}{4} =$ _______

(3) $\dfrac{2}{3} - \dfrac{1}{3} =$ _______

(4) $\dfrac{4}{12} - \dfrac{2}{12} =$ _______

(5) $\dfrac{2}{4} - \dfrac{1}{4} =$ _______

(6) $\dfrac{2}{8} - \dfrac{1}{8} =$ _______

(7) $\dfrac{7}{16} - \dfrac{4}{16} =$ _______

(8) $\dfrac{7}{12} - \dfrac{5}{12} =$ _______

(9) $\dfrac{5}{7} - \dfrac{3}{7} =$ _______

(10) $\dfrac{3}{12} - \dfrac{1}{12} =$ _______

(11) $\dfrac{4}{5} - \dfrac{1}{5} =$ _______

(12) $\dfrac{7}{9} - \dfrac{4}{9} =$ _______

Name: ___________   Date: /   /

A fraction that is less than 1 is called a proper fraction. A fraction that is equal to 1 or greater than 1 is called an improper fraction. **An improper fraction has a numerator equal to or greater than its denominator.**

$\frac{5}{4}$ improper

To change it to a mixed number, you must divide: $5 \div 4$.

$1\frac{1}{4}$

$5 \div 4 = 1$ with a remainder of 1. We write down the 1 as the whole number and the other 1 as the numerator over 4.

To change or convert a mixed fraction to an improper fraction, you **multiply down and add up.**

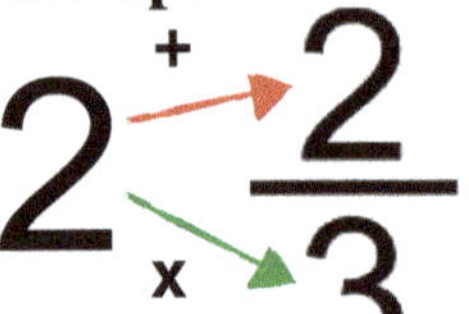

Multiply 2 x 3 = 6

Add 6 + 2 = 8

Write result above the denominator: $\frac{8}{3}$

1 **Practice:**

Convert each to a mixed number or an improper fraction.

(1) $1\frac{1}{3}$ _______

(2) $2\frac{1}{2}$ _______

(3) $\frac{10}{4}$ _______

(4) $2\frac{4}{5}$ _______

(5) $\frac{6}{4}$ _______

(6) $4\frac{5}{6}$ _______

(7) $1\frac{3}{15}$ _______

(8) $3\frac{4}{12}$ _______

(9) $\frac{15}{8}$ _______

(10) $\frac{12}{6}$ _______

(11) $6\frac{3}{9}$ _______

(12) $5\frac{3}{4}$ _______

(13) $8\frac{2}{6}$ _______

(14) $\frac{12}{5}$ _______

Name: ___________   Date: ___ / ___ / ___

To add or subtract fractions that have different denominators, we change one or both of the fractions so that they have common denominators.

The least common multiple (LCM) of the denominators is the least common denominator of the fractions.

$$\frac{1}{2} + \frac{1}{4}$$

We must change 1/2 so that both fractions have a denominator of 4.

$$\frac{1}{2} \times \frac{2}{2} = \frac{2}{4}$$

We ask: "2 times what will give us 4?"

$$\frac{2}{4} + \frac{1}{4} = \frac{3}{4}$$

Now, we can add the numerators to get the answer.

---

1   **Example:**   Add or Subtract the fractions with unlike denominators.

$$\frac{1}{3} \times \frac{4}{4} = \frac{4}{12}$$

$$\frac{4}{12} + \frac{3}{12} = \frac{7}{12}$$

$$+ \; \frac{1}{4} \times \frac{3}{3} = \frac{3}{12}$$

$$\frac{7}{12}$$ ← Answer

$$\frac{1}{2} \times \frac{5}{5} = \frac{5}{10}$$

$$\frac{5}{10} - \frac{2}{10} = \frac{3}{10}$$

$$- \; \frac{1}{5} \times \frac{2}{2} = \frac{2}{10}$$

$$\frac{3}{10}$$ ← Answer

Least Common Multiple (LCM)

3 = 3, 6, (12), 15, 18

4 = 4, (12), 16, 20, 24

Least Common Multiple (LCM)

2 = 2, 4, 6, 8, (10)

5 = 5, (10), 15, 20, 25

$$\frac{1}{2} \xleftrightarrow{+} \frac{1}{4} = \frac{}{2 \times 4} = \frac{}{8}$$

multiply the denominators, 2 x 4

$$\frac{1}{2} \times \frac{1}{4} = \frac{(1 \times 4)+(1 \times 2)}{8} = \frac{4 + 2}{8}$$

now, cross multiply. 1 x 4 and 1 x 2

add

Reduce or simplify the fraction. if needed.

$$\frac{6}{8} \div \frac{2}{2} = \boxed{\frac{3}{4}}$$

$$\frac{1}{2} \xleftrightarrow{-} \frac{1}{5} = \frac{}{2 \times 5} = \frac{}{10}$$

multiply the denominators, 2 x 5

$$\frac{1}{2} \times \frac{1}{5} = \frac{(1 \times 5)-(1 \times 2)}{10} = \frac{5 - 2}{10}$$

now, cross multiply. 1 x 5 and 1 x 2

subtract

Reduce or simplify the fraction. if needed.

$$\boxed{\frac{3}{10}}$$

Practice: Add the fractions with different denominators.

(1) $\dfrac{3}{4} + \dfrac{1}{3} = $ _______

(2) $\dfrac{4}{6} + \dfrac{4}{8} = $ _______

(3) $\dfrac{3}{5} + \dfrac{1}{2} = $ _______

(4) $\dfrac{3}{12} + \dfrac{1}{4} = $ _______

(5) $\dfrac{2}{6} + \dfrac{4}{5} = $ _______

(6) $\dfrac{2}{4} + \dfrac{2}{3} = $ _______

(7) $\dfrac{2}{4} + \dfrac{1}{2} = $ _______

(8) $\dfrac{2}{3} + \dfrac{2}{5} = $ _______

(9) $\dfrac{2}{6} + \dfrac{1}{3} = $ _______

(10) $\dfrac{4}{5} + \dfrac{3}{4} = $ _______

(11) $\dfrac{1}{5} + \dfrac{1}{6} = $ _______

(12) $\dfrac{2}{7} + \dfrac{4}{9} = $ _______

Kamali Academy Fractions

Practice: Subtract the fractions with different denominators.

(1) $\dfrac{5}{6} - \dfrac{8}{12} =$ _______

(2) $\dfrac{3}{4} - \dfrac{2}{8} =$ _______

(3) $\dfrac{2}{3} - \dfrac{1}{4} =$ _______

(4) $\dfrac{4}{5} - \dfrac{2}{12} =$ _______

(5) $\dfrac{2}{4} - \dfrac{1}{3} =$ _______

(6) $\dfrac{2}{4} - \dfrac{1}{8} =$ _______

(7) $\dfrac{5}{4} - \dfrac{4}{9} =$ _______

(8) $\dfrac{3}{4} - \dfrac{5}{12} =$ _______

(9) $\dfrac{5}{7} - \dfrac{1}{5} =$ _______

(10) $\dfrac{6}{2} - \dfrac{1}{3} =$ _______

(11) $\dfrac{4}{5} - \dfrac{3}{7} =$ _______

(12) $\dfrac{7}{9} - \dfrac{3}{5} =$ _______

Name: ___________   Date: /   /

We work with the fraction part of each mixed number first. Then, we add or subtract the whole numbers.

If the denominators are different, they must be made the same. **See the last two lessons for instructions on how to do it.**

$$3\tfrac{3}{6}$$
$$-1\tfrac{1}{6}$$

$$2\tfrac{2}{6}$$ Reduce the fraction.

$$2\tfrac{1}{3}$$

1 **Practice:** Fill in the blank or circle the correct answer.

(1)
$$7\tfrac{1}{12}$$
$$+4\tfrac{8}{12}$$

(4)
$$2\tfrac{2}{3}$$
$$+8\tfrac{3}{4}$$

(2)
$$8\tfrac{2}{3}$$
$$-1\tfrac{1}{3}$$

(5)
$$9\tfrac{1}{6}$$
$$-5\tfrac{1}{3}$$

(3)
$$6\tfrac{1}{4}$$
$$+2\tfrac{1}{4}$$

(6)
$$9\tfrac{2}{5}$$
$$+6\tfrac{7}{10}$$

Kamali Academy Fractions

(1) $4\dfrac{5}{6} - 2\dfrac{8}{12} =$ _____

(2) $5\dfrac{1}{3} - 3\dfrac{2}{4} =$ _____

(3) $2\dfrac{2}{3} + 1\dfrac{1}{4} =$ _____

(4) $5\dfrac{3}{7} + 2\dfrac{1}{7} =$ _____

(5) $3\dfrac{1}{9} - 1\dfrac{5}{9} =$ _____

(6) $3\dfrac{2}{3} - 2\dfrac{2}{5} =$ _____

(7) $1\dfrac{2}{3} + 2\dfrac{2}{5} =$ _____

(8) $1\dfrac{1}{2} + \dfrac{12}{16} =$ _____

(9) $1\dfrac{3}{4} - \dfrac{5}{12} =$ _____

(10) $2\dfrac{2}{6} - 1\dfrac{6}{8} =$ _____

(11) $7\dfrac{5}{6} + 8\dfrac{2}{9} =$ _____

(12) $4\dfrac{4}{8} + 6\dfrac{7}{8} =$ _____

Name: Date: /   /

Section 1: Read the problem carefully and solve. Show your work if you need to.

1. Tutu and Kamau started a lemonade stand to raise money. They donated 2/10 of their profits to their homeschool co-op, 1/10 to the animal shelter, and 4/10 to the food bank. They saved the rest to buy materials for their next project.

   What fraction of their profits did Tutu and Kamau donate?

   ____

2. Abena ate 2 slices of vegan cake. Isata ate 1 slice.

   If Abena ate 2/4 of the cake and all the slices are the same size, what fraction of the cake was eaten in total?

   ____

3. Bakari is baking his favorite dessert. The recipe calls for 5/8 of a cup of butter, but he wants to double the recipe.

   How much butter will Bakari need?

   _______________________ cups

4. Aminu saw a spider with 8 eyes. The spider was looking at him with 2 big front eyes and 3 of its other eyes.

   What fraction of tis eyes were looking at Aminu?

   ____

1. Chike ate 5 slices of pie. Dambasi ate 2 slices.

   If there were initially 10 slices of equal size, what fraction of the pie was eaten?

   ____

2. Jamal and Ife caught a lizard in their backyard. Its length from head to the end of the tail is 43/5 centimeters, and the length of its tail is 16/5 centimeters.

   What is the length of the lizard without the tail?

   ____

3. Malcolm just started high school, and he wants to manage his time wisely. He schedules 3/2 hours each day to his passion, 1/2 of an hour each day for chores at home, and 17/2 hours each day for sleep.

   How many hours each day are scheduled for these activities?

   _____________________ hours

4. Femi worked 87/100 of the problems on her math test in the first hour.

   After the second hour, she had worked 97/100 of the problems.

   What fraction of the problems did she work in the second hour?

   ____

36

Section 1: Read the problem carefully and solve. Show your work if you need to.

1. At the kwanzaa celebration, Ama and her friends at 2 1/2 pizzas. After the celebration, there were 1 1/8 pizzas left.

   How many pizzas were there at the start of the celebration?

   _________________ pizzas

2. Neema bought fabric to make a dress. Yesterday, she used 5/8 of the fabric. Tomorrow, she plans to use another 1/4 of the fabric.

   What fraction of the fabric will she have left after tomorrow?

   _________________ of the fabric

3. At the annual John Carlos and Tommi Smith relay race, the first team member in a 3-person relay race must run 2 1/4 laps, the second team member must run 1 1/2 laps, and the third team member must run 3 5/8 laps.

   How man laps in all must each team run?

   _________________ laps

4. Kantanka played with 3 friends today, all at different times. He played with Tumi for 7/8 of an hour, then Nana for 3/4 of an hour, then Kwesi for 3/2 hours.

   How many hours did Kantanka play with his 3 friends?

   _________________ hours

 **Section 2:** Read the problem carefully and solve. Show your work if you need to.

1. Akua used 2/7 of a meter of kente to make bows for her cousins. Now, she has 10/21 of a meter of kente left.

   How much kente did Akua start with?

   ________________ of a meter

2. Biko's coding class lasts for 5/6 of an hour each day. Today, he has been in the class for 2/5 of an hour so far.

   How much more time is left in the class?

   ________________ of an hour

3. Deandre's fish tank has many different kinds of fish. In particular, 1/6 of the fish are goldfish, and 2/5 of the fish are guppies.

   What fraction of Deandre's fish are either goldfish or guppies?

   ________________ of the fish

4. Nikala and Asante are working at their art gallery. They have sold 1/2 of their art pieces and now have 1/3 of their pieces left to sell.

   What fraction of the art pieces did they start with?

   ________________ art pieces

$$\frac{1}{2} \; \times \; \frac{1}{4} \; = \; \frac{}{8}$$

multiply the denominators, 2 x 4

$$\frac{1}{2} \; \times \; \frac{1}{4} \; = \; \boxed{\frac{1}{8}}$$

multiply. 1 x 1

$$\frac{3}{4} \; \times \; \frac{5}{6} \; = \; \frac{15 \div 3}{24 \div 3} \; = \; \frac{5}{8}$$

reduce

$$1\frac{1}{2} \; \times \; \frac{1}{2} \; = \; \frac{3}{2} \; \times \; \frac{1}{2} \; = \; \boxed{\frac{3}{4}}$$

change to improper first.

$$\frac{2}{5} \; \times \; 5 \; = \; \frac{2}{5} \; \times \; \frac{5}{1} \; = \; \frac{10}{5} \; = \; \boxed{2}$$

rewrite over 1 first   reduce

$$2\frac{1}{4} \; \times \; 1\frac{5}{3} \; = \; \frac{9}{4} \; \times \; \frac{8}{3} \; = \; \frac{72}{12} \; = \; \boxed{6}$$

change to improper fractions   reduce

(1) $\dfrac{1}{2} \times \dfrac{7}{9} = $ _______

(2) $\dfrac{3}{4} \times \dfrac{2}{8} = $ _______

(3) $\dfrac{2}{4} \times \dfrac{1}{4} = $ _______

(4) $\dfrac{2}{5} \times \dfrac{5}{6} = $ _______

(5) $\dfrac{5}{4} \times \dfrac{1}{3} = $ _______

(6) $\dfrac{2}{4} \times \dfrac{5}{7} = $ _______

(7) $\dfrac{4}{9} \times \dfrac{7}{8} = $ _______

(8) $\dfrac{3}{4} \times \dfrac{3}{6} = $ _______

(9) $\dfrac{1}{5} \times \dfrac{1}{3} = $ _______

(10) $\dfrac{6}{7} \times \dfrac{1}{8} = $ _______

(11) $\dfrac{4}{5} \times \dfrac{3}{7} = $ _______

(12) $\dfrac{2}{3} \times \dfrac{3}{5} = $ _______

  Practice: Multiply the fractions. **Of** means multiplication.

(1) $\dfrac{1}{2}$ of $\dfrac{2}{3}$ = _______

(2) $\dfrac{3}{4}$ x $\dfrac{2}{8}$ = _______

(3) $\dfrac{2}{3}$ x $\dfrac{1}{4}$ = _______

(4) $\dfrac{4}{5}$ of $\dfrac{5}{6}$ = _______

(5) $\dfrac{2}{4}$ x $\dfrac{1}{3}$ = _______

(6) $\dfrac{2}{4}$ of $\dfrac{1}{8}$ = _______

(7) $\dfrac{5}{4}$ of $\dfrac{4}{9}$ = _______

(8) $\dfrac{3}{4}$ x $\dfrac{5}{12}$ = _______

(9) $\dfrac{5}{7}$ x $\dfrac{1}{5}$ = _______

(10) $\dfrac{6}{2}$ of $\dfrac{1}{3}$ = _______

(11) $\dfrac{4}{5}$ of $\dfrac{3}{7}$ = _______

(12) $\dfrac{7}{9}$ x $\dfrac{3}{5}$ = _______

   Kamali Academy Fractions

(1) $\dfrac{1}{2} \times 2\dfrac{2}{3} =$ ______

(2) $1\dfrac{1}{5} \times \dfrac{5}{3} =$ ______

(3) $2\dfrac{2}{5}$ of $\dfrac{1}{3} =$ ______

(4) $\dfrac{2}{3} \times 1\dfrac{3}{4} =$ ______

(5) $1\dfrac{1}{5}$ of $1\dfrac{3}{12} =$ ______

(6) $1\dfrac{2}{3} \times 2\dfrac{2}{5} =$ ______

(7) $1\dfrac{1}{2} \times 2\dfrac{1}{2} =$ ______

(8) $1\dfrac{1}{4} \times 2\dfrac{3}{2} =$ ______

(9) $2\dfrac{2}{8} \times 1\dfrac{1}{7} =$ ______

(10) $1\dfrac{3}{7}$ of $\dfrac{11}{5} =$ ______

(11) $1\dfrac{5}{6} \times 2\dfrac{2}{5} =$ ______

(12) $2\dfrac{1}{4} \times 1\dfrac{2}{6} =$ ______

Name: Date: /   /

Section 1: Read the problem carefully and solve. Show your work if you need to.

---

1. Akosua bought 9 yam balls and ate 1/3 of them.
   Fulani bought 6 yam balls and ate 2/3 of them.

   Who ate more yam balls? (choose 1 answer)

   (A) Akosua   (B) Fulani   (C) They ate the same number of yam balls.

2. 1/3 of the students in Mrs. Mansaray's class have dogs. Of those
   students, 2/5 have beagles.

   What fraction of the students in Mrs. Mansaray's class have beagles?

   _________________ of the students

3. Aisha spent 1 1/2 hours on the beach. She fell asleep for 3/4 of the
   time she was on the beach when her mom woke her up.

   How many hours was Aisha asleep on the beach?

   _______________ hours

4. Kumani took a quiz on African geography that had 15 questions. She
   got 4/5 of those questions correct.

   She took another quiz on Senegalese history that had 12 questions.
   She got 5/6 of those questions correct.

   One which quiz did Kumani get more questions correct?

   (A) Geography quiz   (B) Senegalese quiz

1. Nataki spent 2/3 of her time at the basketball court working on her shooting. She spent 7/8 of her shooting time on standstill shots.

   What fraction of her shooting workout did she spend on standstill shots?

   ____

2. Toure's brother is 1 1/2 meters tall. Toure is 3/5 of his brother's height.

   How tall is Toure?

   _______________ meters

3. Oya's pet store has 20 animals, and 2/5 of them are puppies.

   Rafiki's pet store has 12 animals, and 3/4 of them are puppies.

   Which pet store has more puppies?

   (A) Oya's   (B) Rafiki's   (C) Each store has the same number

4. Selasi spent 1/2 of the day hiking. He was lost 5/6 of the time that he was hiking.

   What fraction of the day was Selasi lost?

   _______________ of the day

Name: ___________   Date: __ / __ / __

Fractions are nothing more than division questions.
They can be written as a division question as well.

$\dfrac{3}{6}$ is the same as $3 \div 6$

$1 \div 2$ is the same as $\dfrac{1}{2}$

1 **Practice:** Fill in the blank or circle the correct answer.

(1) $\dfrac{3}{4} = 3 \div \underline{\qquad}$

(2) $\dfrac{5}{7} = 5 \div \underline{\qquad}$

(3) $3 \div 12 =$

(a) $\dfrac{3}{8}$ (c) $\dfrac{8}{3}$

(b) $\dfrac{3}{12}$ (d) $\dfrac{12}{5}$

(4) $\dfrac{6}{5} = 6 \div \underline{\qquad}$

(5) $\dfrac{2}{6} = 2 \div \underline{\qquad}$

(6) $4 \div 7 =$

(a) $\dfrac{7}{4}$ (c) $\dfrac{4}{7}$

(b) $\dfrac{3}{7}$ (d) $\dfrac{4}{9}$

(7) $\dfrac{5}{9} = 5 \div \underline{\qquad}$

(8) $\dfrac{4}{5} = 4 \div \underline{\qquad}$

(9) $8 \div 15 =$

(a) $\dfrac{6}{8}$ (c) $\dfrac{13}{8}$

(b) $\dfrac{15}{8}$ (d) $\dfrac{8}{15}$

Kamali Academy Fractions

Name: ___________ Date: ___ / ___ / ___

When dividing fractions by whole numbers, **make the whole number into a fraction by putting it over 1.**
Then, **change the sign to multiplication and flip the second to its <u>reciprocal</u>.**

$$\frac{1}{2} \div 3 \implies \frac{1}{2} \div \frac{3}{1}$$

$$\frac{1}{2} \times \frac{1}{3}$$

Now, change the sign and flip the 3/1. Multiply across. $= \frac{1}{6}$

---

1 **Practice:** Divide the whole numbers.

(1) $\dfrac{1}{5} \div 3 = $ ______

(2) $\dfrac{1}{9} \div 8 = $ ______

(3) $\dfrac{1}{7} \div 10 = $ ______

(4) $\dfrac{1}{2} \div 9 = $ ______

(5) $\dfrac{1}{9} \div 2 = $ ______

(6) $4 \div \dfrac{1}{5} = $ ______

(7) $\dfrac{1}{3} \div 5 = $ ______

(8) $4 \div \dfrac{1}{3} = $ ______

(9) $\dfrac{1}{8} \div 6 = $ ______

(10) $4 \div \dfrac{1}{4} = $ ______

(11) $\dfrac{1}{7} \div 6 = $ ______

(12) $8 \div \dfrac{1}{2} = $ ______

(1) $\dfrac{3}{4} \div \dfrac{3}{4} =$ _______

(2) $\dfrac{1}{2} \div \dfrac{2}{5} =$ _______

(3) $\dfrac{2}{4} \div \dfrac{1}{4} =$ _______

(4) $\dfrac{4}{9} \div \dfrac{5}{6} =$ _______

(5) $\dfrac{1}{3} \div \dfrac{6}{9} =$ _______

(6) $\dfrac{2}{4} \div \dfrac{5}{7} =$ _______

(7) $\dfrac{5}{10} \div \dfrac{7}{8} =$ _______

(8) $\dfrac{3}{6} \div \dfrac{3}{4} =$ _______

(9) $\dfrac{1}{5} \div \dfrac{1}{3} =$ _______

(10) $\dfrac{3}{8} \div \dfrac{7}{8} =$ _______

(11) $\dfrac{1}{4} \div \dfrac{1}{7} =$ _______

(12) $\dfrac{8}{10} \div \dfrac{2}{5} =$ _______

 Practice: Divide the fractions.

(1) $\dfrac{8}{12} \div \dfrac{7}{8} = $ _______

(2) $\dfrac{3}{4} \div \dfrac{4}{5} = $ _______

(3) $\dfrac{4}{5} \div \dfrac{1}{4} = $ _______

(4) $\dfrac{1}{2} \div \dfrac{2}{3} = $ _______

(5) $\dfrac{2}{4} \div \dfrac{2}{5} = $ _______

(6) $\dfrac{2}{4} \div \dfrac{1}{8} = $ _______

(7) $\dfrac{1}{2} \div \dfrac{5}{6} = $ _______

(8) $\dfrac{2}{7} \div \dfrac{4}{9} = $ _______

(9) $\dfrac{5}{7} \div \dfrac{1}{5} = $ _______

(10) $\dfrac{5}{7} \div \dfrac{3}{7} = $ _______

(11) $\dfrac{1}{3} \div \dfrac{4}{5} = $ _______

(12) $\dfrac{1}{10} \div \dfrac{5}{6} = $ _______

48

Kamali Academy Fractions

Name: Date: /   /

Change the mixed numbers into an improper fractions first.
Then, **change the sign and flip the second fraction to its <u>reciprocal</u>.**

$$1\frac{1}{2} \div 1\frac{1}{3} \;\Rightarrow\; \frac{3}{2} \div \frac{4}{3}$$

$$\frac{3}{2} \Rightarrow \;\times\; \frac{3}{4}$$

Now, change the sign and flip to 3/4. Multiply across. $= \frac{9}{8}$

① Practice: Divide the whole numbers.

(1) $\quad 1\frac{1}{4} \div 1\frac{2}{5} \;=\; \dfrac{25}{28}$ _______

(2) $\quad 12 \div 1\frac{1}{5} \;=\;$ _______

(3) $\quad 8 \div 1\frac{4}{5} \;=\;$ _______

(4) $\quad 1\frac{7}{9} \div \frac{4}{5} \;=\;$ _______

(5) $\quad 4\frac{2}{3} \div \frac{1}{2} \;=\;$ _______

(6) $\quad \frac{5}{8} \div 1\frac{1}{3} \;=\;$ _______

(7) $\quad \frac{3}{5} \div 2\frac{1}{2} \;=\;$ _______

(8) $\quad 5\frac{2}{3} \div 4 \;=\;$ _______

(9) $\quad 4\frac{2}{3} \div 7 \;=\;$ _______

(10) $\quad 3\frac{2}{4} \div 1\frac{1}{3} \;=\;$ _______

(11) $\quad 2\frac{1}{2} \div 2\frac{2}{3} \;=\;$ _______

(12) $\quad 3\frac{3}{4} \div \frac{5}{7} \;=\;$ _______

Kamali Academy Fractions

(1)
$$4\frac{1}{2} \div 6 = \underline{\hspace{2cm}}$$

(2)
$$2\frac{4}{5} \div 1\frac{3}{4} = \underline{\hspace{2cm}}$$

(3)
$$3\frac{1}{5} \div 1\frac{3}{5} = \underline{\hspace{2cm}}$$

(4)
$$\frac{5}{6} \div 2\frac{1}{3} = \underline{\hspace{2cm}}$$

(5)
$$3\frac{2}{3} \div 4 = \underline{\hspace{2cm}}$$

(6)
$$7\frac{1}{2} \div 4\frac{1}{2} = \underline{\hspace{2cm}}$$

(7)
$$2\frac{5}{10} \div 2\frac{5}{8} = \underline{\hspace{2cm}}$$

(8)
$$\frac{3}{6} \div 3\frac{3}{4} = \underline{\hspace{2cm}}$$

(9)
$$2\frac{6}{7} \div 5 = \underline{\hspace{2cm}}$$

(10)
$$4\frac{2}{5} \div 1\frac{1}{10} = \underline{\hspace{2cm}}$$

(11)
$$7\frac{1}{5} \div 3\frac{1}{5} = \underline{\hspace{2cm}}$$

(12)
$$\frac{2}{3} \div 2\frac{2}{9} = \underline{\hspace{2cm}}$$

Name: _______________   Date: ___ / ___ / ___

Section 1: Read the problem carefully and solve. Show your work if you need to.

1. A relay race covers 1 1/2 miles, and each runner on a team will run 1/4 of a mile.

   How many runners are needed for a team?

   ___________________ runners

2. A seal can walk 1/12 of a kilometer in an hour. The seal is 1/5 of a mile away from the ocean.

   At this speed, how long will it take the seal to reach the ocean?

   ___________________ hours

3. The djembe teacher has 4 1/2 hours available to teach in a night. Each lesson will last 1 1/2 hours.

   How many lessons can the teacher schedule in a night?

   ___________________ lessons

4. Ashonta is using her phone. Its battery life is down to 2/5, and it drains another 1/9 every hour.

   How many hours will her battery last?

   ___________________ hours

 **Section 2:** Read the problem carefully and solve. Show your work if you need to.

1. The African gourmet chef has 5 1/4 pies in her shop. She cut the pies in pieces that are each 1/8 of a whole pie.

   How many pieces of pie does she have?

   _________________ pieces

2. A 16 1/2 mile stretch of road needs repairs. Workers can repair 2 1/4 mile of road per week.

   How many weeks will it take to repair this stretch of road?

   _________________ weeks

3. Seti has some cookies that he wants to give away. He is going to give each person 1/8 of a box, and he has 2 3/4 boxes to give away.

   How many people will get cookies?

   _________________ people

4. Imani can run 1/6 of a mile in a minute. Her homeschool co-op is 3/4 of a mile away from her home.

   At this speed, how long would it take Imani to run home from the homeschool co-op?

   _________________ minutes

Notes:

Notes:

Answer Key:

Chapter 1 Naming Fractions:
Section 2 Practice
1. 2/3
2. 1/3
3. 2/5
4. 2/5
5. 2/3
6. 4/6
7. 1/5
8. 3/5
9. 1/6
10. 3/5
11. 3/8
12. 4/8
13. 1/2
14. 2/6
15. 1/5

Section 3 Practice
1. 1/3
2. 1/4
3. 1/4
4. 2/5
5. 1/4
6. 3/5
7. 3/4
8. 2/4
9. 3/6
10. 2/6
11. 2/3
12. 4/6
13. 4/9
14. 2/4
15. 7/8

Section 4 Practice
1. 4
2. 9
3. 9
4. 7
5. 4
6. 9
7. 2
8. 4
9. 8
10. 1
11. 8
12. 3
13. 3
14. 8
15. 2
16. 8
17. 4
18. 4
19. 4
20. 1
21. 8
22. 8
23. 5
24. 7
25. 8
26. 7

Chapter 3 Writing Fractions in Words
Section 1
1. two thirds
2. one tenths
3. one half
4. three sevenths
5. four fifths
6. eight twelfths
7. eight ninths
8. five sixths
9. five eighths
10. two fifths
11. six twelfths
12. seven tenths
13. two ninths
14. two sixths
15. eleven twelfths
16. five sevenths

Section 2
1. 1/3
2. 1/2
3. 1/6
4. 2/5
5. 4/7
6. 7/8
7. 5/12
8. 8/9
9. 6/10
10. 8/6
11. 7/12
12. 1/5
13. 1/11
14. 8/9
15. 6/10
16. 6/12
17. 5/6
18. 2/7
19. 2/3
20. 5/13

Chapter 5 Understanding Mixed Numbers
Section 1
1. 2 ¾
2. 3 2/3
3. 2 2/8
4. 1 4/5
5. 2 ½
6. 2 2/3
7. 1 2/4
8. 3 3/6
9. 1 1/3
10. 4 ½
11. 2 5/6
12. 3 ¼
13. 2 1/8
14. 1 ½
15. 3 2/3
16. 4 1/3

Section 2
1. two and two thirds
2. five and one tenths
3. eight and one half
4. three and three sevenths
5. five and four fifths
6. one and eight twelfths
7. two and eight ninths
8. seven and five sixths
9. one and five eighths
10. three and two fifths
11. seven and six twelfths
12. one and seven tenths
13. eight and two ninths
14. two and two sixths
15. eight and eleven twelfths
16. one and five sevenths

Chapter 7 Equivalent Fractions
Section 1
1. 3/3
2. 2/2
3. 4/4
4. 5/5
5. 2/2
6. 2/2
7. 4/4
8. 2/2
9. 5/5
10. 2/2
11. 3/3
12. 4/4

Section 2
1. 10
2. 6
3. 9
4. 2
5. 4
6. 3
7. 5
8. 16
9. 10
10. 4
11. 8
12. 4

Chapter 8 Compare Fractions
Section 1
1. >
2. >
3. <
4. <
5. >
6. >
7. <
8. >
9. <
10. >
11. >
12. >
13. >
14. <
15. <
16. >

Chapter 9 Compare Fractions
Section 1
1. <
2. =
3. <
4. <
5. <
6. >
7. >
8. >
9. >
10. =
11. >
12. <
13. <
14. >
15. <
16. <

Chapter 12 Simplify Fractions
Section 1
1. ½
2. 1/3
3. 3/7
4. ¾
5. ½
6. 7/9
7. 2/7
8. 3/5
9. 8/7
10. 8/7
11. 2/5
12. 7/9
13. 3/2
14. 3/5
15. 5/4
16. 9/5
17. 1/3
18. 3/4
19. 4
20. 8/13
21. 1/10
22. 5/4
23. 5/3
24. 1/3

Chapter 13 Adding and Subtracting Fractions
Section 1
1. 5/8
2. 4/9
3. 3/5
4. 2/7
5. 5/6
6. 1/2
7. 7/12
8. 2/3
9. 6/7
10. 9/8
11. 1
12. 2/3

Section 2
1. 2
2. 5/12
3. 1
4. 2/3
5. ½
6. 10/3
7. 11/4
8. 1
9. 11/2
10. 1/3
11. 1
12. 11/9

Section 3
1. ½
2. ¼
3. 1/3
4. 1/6
5. ¼
6. 1/8
7. 3/16
8. 1/6
9. 2/7
10. 1/6
11. 3/5
12. 1/3

Chapter 14 Rewrite Mixed Numbers
Section 1
1. 4/3
2. 5/2
3. 2 ½
4. 14/5
5. 1 ½
6. 29/6
7. 6/5
8. 10/3
9. 1 7/8
10. 2
11. 57/9
12. 23/4
13. 50/6
14. 2 2/5

Chapter 16 Adding and Subtracting Fractions
Section 1
1. 1 1/12
2. 1 1/6
3. 1 1/10
4. ½
5. 1 2/15
6. 1 1/6
7. 1
8. 1 1/15
9. 2/3
10. 1 11/20
11. 11/30
12. 46/63

Section 2
1. 1/12
2. ½
3. 5/12
4. 19/30
5. 1/6
6. 3/8
7. 29/36
8. 1/3
9. 18/35
10. 2 2/3
11. 13/35
12. 8/45

Chapter 17 Adding and Subtracting Mixed Numbers
Section 1
1. 11 ¾
2. 7 1/3
3. 8 ½
4. 11 5/12
5. 3 5/6
6. 16 1/10

Section 2
1. 2 1/12
2. 1 5/6
3. 3 11/12
4. 7 4/7
5. 1 5/9
6. 1 4/15
7. 4 1/15
8. 2 ¼
9. 1 1/3
10. 7/12
11. 15 11/18
12. 11 3/8

Chapter 18 Add and Subtract Word Problems
Section 1
1. 7/10
2. ¾
3. 10/8 or 2 ¼
4. 5/8

Section 2
1. 7/10
2. 27/5
3. 21/2
4. 10/100 or 1/10

Chapter 19 Add and Subtraction Word Problems
Section 1
1. 3 5/8
2. 1/8
3. 7 3/8
4. 27/8 or 3 3/8 hours

Section 2
1. 16/21
2. 13/30
3. 17/30
4. 5/6

Chapter 20 Multiplying Fractions
Section 2
1. 7/18
2. 3/16
3. 1/8
4. 1/3
5. 5/12
6. 5/14
7. 7/18
8. 3/8
9. 1/15
10. 3/28
11. 12/35
12. 6/15

Section 3
1. 1/3
2. 3/16
3. 1/6
4. 2/3
5. 1/6
6. 1/16
7. 5/9
8. 5/16
9. 1/7
10. 1
11. 12/35
12. 7/15

Section 4
1. 1 1/3
2. 2
3. 4/5
4. 1 1/6
5. 1 1/2
6. 4
7. 3 ¾
8. 4 3/8
9. 2 4/7
10. 3 1/7
11. 4 2/5
12. 3

Chapter 21 Multiplying Fraction Word Problems
Section 1
1. B
2. 2/15
3. 9/8 or 1 1/8
4. A

Section 2
1. 7/12
2. 9/10
3. B
4. 5/12

Chapter 22 Fractions as Division
Section 1
1. 4
2. 7
3. B
4. 5
5. 6
6. C
7. 9
8. 5
9. D

Chapter 23 Dividing Unit Fractions by Whole Numbers
Section 1
1. 1/15
2. 1/72
3. 1/18
4. 1/18
5. 1/18
6. 20
7. 1/15
8. 12
9. 1/48
10. 16
11. 1/42
12. 16

Section 2
1. 1
2. 5/4
3. 2
4. 8/15
5. ½
6. 7/10
7. 4/7
8. 2/3
9. 3/5
10. 3/7
11. 7/4 or 1 ¾
12. 2

Section 3
1. 16/21
2. 15/16
3. 16/5 or 3 1/5
4. ¾
5. 10/8 or 1 ¼
6. 4
7. 3/5
8. 9/14
9. 25/7 or 3 4/7
10. 5/3 or 1 2/3
11. 5/12
12. 3/25

Chapter 24 Dividing Mixed Numbers
Section 1
1. 25/28
2. 10
3. 40/9 or 4 4/9
4. 2 2/9
5. 28/3 or 9 1/3
6. 15/32
7. 12/25
8. 17/12 or 1 5/12
9. 2/3
10. 2 5/8
11. 15/14 or 1 1/14
12. 5 ¼

Section 2
1. ¾
2. 1 3/5
3. 2
4. 5/14
5. 11/12
6. 1 2/3
7. 20/21
8. 2/15
9. 4/7
10. 4
11. 2 ¼
12. 3/10

Chapter 25 Dividing Fractions Word Problems
Section 1
1. 6
2. 2 2/5
3. 3
4. 3 3/5

Section 2
1. 42
2. 7 1/3
3. 22
4. 4 1/2